BIBLIOPHILE

A READER'S JOURNAL

by Jane Mount

CHRONICLE BOOKS

SAN FRANCISCO

ISBN 978-1-4521-6731-2

Manufactured in China.

MIX
Paper from
responsible sources
FSC
www.fsc.org
FSC™ C008047

Design by Kristen Hewitt.
Typeset in Brandon Text.

10 9 8 7 6 5 4

Chronicle Books LLC
680 Second Street
San Francisco, California 94107
www.chroniclebooks.com

INTRODUCTION

When I was a kid I was super shy and weird and had few
friends, so I read books to escape. One summer, I convinced
my dad to drop me off at the public library instead of day
camp (thank you, kind librarians!). I would read at least one
book before he walked over for our lunch and one book after.
By August I had crushed the Summer Reading Program; the
rocket ship–shaped, construction-paper cutout on the wall
with my name on it was packed with gold stars. And I had
begun to learn a little something from all those books about
how to connect to others. Books make us better people.

This journal is your reading program, but way
better. Log in each book you read, record your
thoughts and favorite quotes, and get inspired
for your next literary journey. Every page you
complete is a giant gold star, and every book
you read will help you become a better person.

This is my favorite book!
(Bullseye Books
1996 paperback)

BOOK NOTES

DATE STARTED

/   /

DATE FINISHED

/   /

RATE THIS BOOK

☆☆☆☆☆

BOOK TITLE:

AUTHOR:

Plot notes:

Character notes:

Favorite quotes:

Other books to read by this author:

BOOK TITLE: _____

_____

AUTHOR: _____

_____

_____

Plot notes: _____

_____

_____

_____

_____

Character notes: _____

_____

_____

_____

_____

Favorite quotes: _____

_____

_____

_____

_____

Other books to read by this author: _____

_____

BOOKS MADE INTO GREAT MOVIES

BOOK TITLE:

AUTHOR:

Plot notes:

Character notes:

Favorite quotes:

Other books to read by this author:

DATE STARTED

/ /

DATE FINISHED

/ /

RATE THIS BOOK

☆☆☆☆☆

BOOK TITLE: _____

_____

AUTHOR: _____

_____

Plot notes: _____

_____

_____

_____

_____

Character notes: _____

_____

_____

_____

_____

Favorite quotes: _____

_____

_____

_____

_____

Other books to read by this author: _____

_____

BOOK TITLE: _____

AUTHOR: _____

_____

Plot notes: _____

_____

_____

_____

_____

_____

Character notes: _____

_____

_____

_____

_____

Favorite quotes: _____

_____

_____

_____

_____

Other books to read by this author: _____

_____

DATE STARTED

/   /

DATE FINISHED

/   /

RATE THIS BOOK

☆ ☆ ☆ ☆ ☆

DATE STARTED

/   /

DATE FINISHED

/   /

RATE THIS BOOK

☆☆☆☆☆

BOOK TITLE:

AUTHOR:

Plot notes:

Character notes:

Favorite quotes:

Other books to read by this author:

BOOK TITLE: _____

_____

AUTHOR: _____

_____

_____

Plot notes: _____

_____

_____

_____

_____

Character notes: _____

_____

_____

_____

Favorite quotes: _____

_____

_____

_____

Other books to read by this author: _____

_____

DATE STARTED

/   /

DATE FINISHED

/   /

RATE THIS BOOK

☆☆☆☆☆

BOOK TITLE:

AUTHOR:

Plot notes:

Character notes:

Favorite quotes:

Other books to read by this author:

DATE STARTED

/   /

DATE FINISHED

/   /

RATE THIS BOOK

☆☆☆☆☆

BOOK TITLE:

AUTHOR:

Plot notes:

Character notes:

Favorite quotes:

Other books to read by this author:

BOOK TITLE: _____

_____

AUTHOR: _____

_____

Plot notes: _____

_____

_____

_____

_____

Character notes: _____

_____

_____

_____

_____

Favorite quotes: _____

_____

_____

_____

_____

Other books to read by this author: _____

_____

DATE STARTED

/   /

DATE FINISHED

/   /

RATE THIS BOOK

☆ ☆ ☆ ☆ ☆

DATE STARTED

/　　/

DATE FINISHED

/　　/

RATE THIS BOOK

☆☆☆☆☆

BOOK TITLE:

AUTHOR:

Plot notes:

Character notes:

Favorite quotes:

Other books to read by this author:

BOOK TITLE: _____

_____

AUTHOR: _____

_____

_____

Plot notes: _____

_____

_____

_____

_____

Character notes: _____

_____

_____

_____

_____

Favorite quotes: _____

_____

_____

_____

_____

Other books to read by this author: _____

_____

DATE STARTED

/   /

DATE FINISHED

/   /

RATE THIS BOOK

☆ ☆ ☆ ☆ ☆

JANE AUSTEN'S WRITING ROOM

Chawton Cottage, Hampshire

Austen's walnut dodecagon writing desk

Small framed silhouettes of Austen's parents.

Austen's small gold ring with a turquoise stone

BOOK TITLE:_____
_____

AUTHOR:_____
_____

Plot notes:_____
_____
_____
_____
_____

Character notes:_____
_____
_____
_____

Favorite quotes:_____
_____
_____
_____

Other books to read by this author:_____
_____

DATE STARTED

/   /

DATE FINISHED

/   /

RATE THIS BOOK

☆☆☆☆☆

DATE STARTED

/   /

DATE FINISHED

/   /

RATE THIS BOOK

☆ ☆ ☆ ☆ ☆

BOOK TITLE:_____

_____

AUTHOR:_____

_____

_____

Plot notes: _____

_____

_____

_____

_____

_____

Character notes: _____

_____

_____

_____

_____

Favorite quotes: _____

_____

_____

_____

_____

Other books to read by this author: _____

_____

BOOK TITLE: _____

_____

AUTHOR: _____

_____

_____

Plot notes: _____

_____

_____

_____

_____

Character notes: _____

_____

_____

_____

Favorite quotes: _____

_____

_____

_____

Other books to read by this author: _____

_____

DATE STARTED

/   /

DATE FINISHED

/   /

RATE THIS BOOK

☆☆☆☆☆

BOOK TITLE:

AUTHOR:

Plot notes:

Character notes:

Favorite quotes:

Other books to read by this author:

BOOK TITLE: _____

_____

AUTHOR: _____

_____

_____

Plot notes: _____

_____

_____

_____

_____

Character notes: _____

_____

_____

_____

_____

Favorite quotes: _____

_____

_____

_____

Other books to read by this author: _____

_____

DATE STARTED

/   /

DATE FINISHED

/   /

RATE THIS BOOK

☆ ☆ ☆ ☆ ☆

DATE STARTED

/   /

DATE FINISHED

/   /

RATE THIS BOOK

☆☆☆☆☆

BOOK TITLE:

AUTHOR:

Plot notes:

Character notes:

Favorite quotes:

Other books to read by this author:

The very first edition ever! Titles were not on covers in those days. The initial print run was 1,500 copies, and they cost 18 shillings each.

One of a large set of Penguin Clothbound Classics, all designed by the ridiculously talented Coralie Bickford-Smith.

DATE STARTED

/   /

DATE FINISHED

/   /

RATE THIS BOOK

☆☆☆☆☆

BOOK TITLE: _____

_____

AUTHOR: _____

_____

Plot notes: _____

_____

_____

_____

_____

_____

Character notes: _____

_____

_____

_____

Favorite quotes: _____

_____

_____

_____

Other books to read by this author: _____

_____

BOOK TITLE: _____

_____

AUTHOR: _____

_____

Plot notes: _____

_____

_____

_____

_____

Character notes: _____

_____

_____

_____

Favorite quotes: _____

_____

_____

_____

Other books to read by this author: _____

_____

DATE STARTED

/ /

DATE FINISHED

/ /

RATE THIS BOOK

☆ ☆ ☆ ☆ ☆

BOOK TITLE: _____

_____

AUTHOR: _____

_____

Plot notes: _____

_____
_____
_____
_____

Character notes: _____

_____
_____
_____
_____

Favorite quotes: _____

_____
_____
_____
_____

Other books to read by this author: _____

_____

BOOK TITLE: _____

_____

AUTHOR: _____

_____

_____

Plot notes: _____

_____

_____

_____

_____

Character notes: _____

_____

_____

_____

_____

Favorite quotes: _____

_____

_____

_____

_____

Other books to read by this author: _____

_____

DATE STARTED

/   /

DATE FINISHED

/   /

RATE THIS BOOK

☆☆☆☆☆

BOOK TITLE: _____

_____

AUTHOR: _____

_____

_____

Plot notes: _____

_____

_____

_____

_____

Character notes: _____

_____

_____

_____

Favorite quotes: _____

_____

_____

_____

Other books to read by this author: _____

_____

DATE STARTED

/ /

DATE FINISHED

/ /

RATE THIS BOOK

☆☆☆☆☆

DATE STARTED

/   /

DATE FINISHED

/   /

RATE THIS BOOK

☆☆☆☆☆

BOOK TITLE:_____

_____

AUTHOR:_____

_____

_____

Plot notes:_____

_____

_____

_____

_____

_____

Character notes:_____

_____

_____

_____

_____

Favorite quotes:_____

_____

_____

_____

_____

Other books to read by this author:_____

_____

BOOK TITLE: _____
_____

AUTHOR: _____
_____

Plot notes: _____
_____
_____
_____
_____

Character notes: _____
_____
_____
_____
_____

Favorite quotes: _____
_____
_____
_____
_____

Other books to read by this author: _____
_____

DATE STARTED

/   /

DATE FINISHED

/   /

RATE THIS BOOK

☆☆☆☆☆

DATE STARTED

/ /

DATE FINISHED

/ /

RATE THIS BOOK

☆☆☆☆☆

BOOK TITLE:

AUTHOR:

Plot notes:

Character notes:

Favorite quotes:

Other books to read by this author:

BOOK TITLE:

AUTHOR:

Plot notes:

Character notes:

Favorite quotes:

Other books to read by this author:

DATE STARTED

/ /

DATE FINISHED

/ /

RATE THIS BOOK

☆☆☆☆☆

BOOK TITLE:

AUTHOR:

Plot notes:

Character notes:

Favorite quotes:

Other books to read by this author:

NOVEL FOOD

Perfect Key lime pie for throwing at an ex-husband from "Heartburn" by Nora Ephron

Not enough gruel from "Oliver Twist" by Charles Dickens

Buttered yams from a Harlem street vendor from "Invisible Man" by Ralph Ellison

Mom's madeleines and tea from "Swann's Way" by Marcel Proust

Irresistible Turkish delight from "The Lion, the Witch, and the Wardrobe" by C. S. Lewis

Pasta puttanesca hated by Count Olaf in "A Series of Unfortunate Events: The Bad Beginning" by Lemony Snicket

Avocado with crab salad (and food poisoning) from "The Bell Jar" by Sylvia Plath

Butterbeer and Bertie Bott's Every Flavor Beans from "Harry Potter and the Sorcerer's Stone" by J.K. Rowling

Yet another apple pie with ice cream from "On the Road" by Jack Kerouac

Unlucky crab missing a leg from "The Joy Luck Club" by Amy Tan

DATE STARTED

/ /

DATE FINISHED

/ /

RATE THIS BOOK

☆☆☆☆☆

BOOK TITLE:

AUTHOR:

Plot notes:

Character notes:

Favorite quotes:

Other books to read by this author:

BOOK TITLE:

AUTHOR:

Plot notes:

Character notes:

Favorite quotes:

Other books to read by this author:

DATE STARTED

/   /

DATE FINISHED

/   /

RATE THIS BOOK

☆ ☆ ☆ ☆ ☆

DATE STARTED

/   /

DATE FINISHED

/   /

RATE THIS BOOK

☆☆☆☆☆

BOOK TITLE:

AUTHOR:

Plot notes:

Character notes:

Favorite quotes:

Other books to read by this author:

BOOK TITLE: _____

_____

AUTHOR: _____

_____

_____

Plot notes: _____

_____

_____

_____

_____

_____

Character notes: _____

_____

_____

_____

_____

Favorite quotes: _____

_____

_____

_____

_____

Other books to read by this author: _____

_____

DATE STARTED

/   /

DATE FINISHED

/   /

RATE THIS BOOK

☆ ☆ ☆ ☆ ☆

HENRY DAVID THOREAU'S WRITING ROOM

Thoreau spent $28.12 on materials for his 10' x 15' cabin. It was built from wood he split with the help of friends and the remains of a shanty he bought from an Irish railroad worker and disassembled.

Today, near Concord, Massachusetts, short stone columns mark where the cabin's chimney and four corners originally stood.

A replica of the cabin sits closer to the parking lot of what's now Walden Pond State Reservation. Countless other replicas have been constructed, including one built in protest of a gas pipeline, a tribute to Thoreau's ideals about wilderness.

BOOK TITLE: _____

_____

AUTHOR: _____

_____

_____

Plot notes: _____

_____

_____

_____

_____

_____

Character notes: _____

_____

_____

_____

_____

Favorite quotes: _____

_____

_____

_____

_____

Other books to read by this author: _____

_____

DATE STARTED

/   /

DATE FINISHED

/   /

RATE THIS BOOK

☆ ☆ ☆ ☆ ☆

DATE STARTED

/ /

DATE FINISHED

/ /

RATE THIS BOOK

☆☆☆☆☆

BOOK TITLE:

AUTHOR:

Plot notes:

Character notes:

Favorite quotes:

Other books to read by this author:

BOOK TITLE:

AUTHOR:

Plot notes:

Character notes:

Favorite quotes:

Other books to read by this author:

DATE STARTED

/ /

DATE FINISHED

/ /

RATE THIS BOOK

☆☆☆☆☆

BOOK TITLE: _____

_____

AUTHOR: _____

_____

_____

Plot notes: _____

_____

_____

_____

_____

_____

Character notes: _____

_____

_____

_____

_____

Favorite quotes: _____

_____

_____

_____

_____

Other books to read by this author: _____

_____

BOOK TITLE: _____

_____

AUTHOR: _____

_____

_____

Plot notes: _____

_____

_____

_____

_____

Character notes: _____

_____

_____

_____

Favorite quotes: _____

_____

_____

_____

Other books to read by this author: _____

_____

DATE STARTED

/   /

DATE FINISHED

/   /

RATE THIS BOOK

☆ ☆ ☆ ☆ ☆

DATE STARTED

/   /

DATE FINISHED

/   /

RATE THIS BOOK

☆☆☆☆☆

BOOK TITLE:

AUTHOR:

Plot notes:

Character notes:

Favorite quotes:

Other books to read by this author:

DATE STARTED

/   /

DATE FINISHED

/   /

RATE THIS BOOK

☆☆☆☆☆

BOOK TITLE: _____
_____

AUTHOR: _____
_____
_____

Plot notes: _____
_____
_____
_____
_____
_____

Character notes: _____
_____
_____
_____
_____

Favorite quotes: _____
_____
_____
_____
_____

Other books to read by this author: ___
_____

BOOK TITLE: _____

_____

AUTHOR: _____

_____

_____

Plot notes: _____

_____

_____

_____

_____

Character notes: _____

_____

_____

_____

Favorite quotes: _____

_____

_____

_____

Other books to read by this author: _____

_____

DATE STARTED

/ /

DATE FINISHED

/ /

RATE THIS BOOK

☆☆☆☆☆

DATE STARTED	**BOOK TITLE:** _____
/ /	_____
DATE FINISHED	**AUTHOR:** _____
/ /	_____
RATE THIS BOOK	
☆☆☆☆☆	**Plot notes:** _____

_____

_____

_____

_____

_____

Character notes: _____

_____

_____

_____

Favorite quotes: _____

_____

_____

_____

Other books to read by this author: _____

_____

BOOK TITLE:

AUTHOR:

DATE STARTED

/   /

DATE FINISHED

/   /

RATE THIS BOOK

☆ ☆ ☆ ☆ ☆

Plot notes:

Character notes:

Favorite quotes:

Other books to read by this author:

BOOKSTORE CATS

BOOK TITLE: _____

_____

AUTHOR: _____

_____

_____

Plot notes: _____

_____

_____

_____

_____

Character notes: _____

_____

_____

_____

_____

Favorite quotes: _____

_____

_____

_____

_____

Other books to read by this author: _____

_____

DATE STARTED

/ /

DATE FINISHED

/ /

RATE THIS BOOK

☆☆☆☆☆

DATE STARTED

/ /

DATE FINISHED

/ /

RATE THIS BOOK

☆☆☆☆☆

BOOK TITLE:

AUTHOR:

Plot notes:

Character notes:

Favorite quotes:

Other books to read by this author:

BOOK TITLE:

AUTHOR:

Plot notes:

Character notes:

Favorite quotes:

Other books to read by this author:

DATE STARTED

/   /

DATE FINISHED

/   /

RATE THIS BOOK

☆☆☆☆☆

BOOK TITLE:

AUTHOR:

Plot notes:

Character notes:

Favorite quotes:

Other books to read by this author:

BOOK TITLE: _____

_____

AUTHOR: _____

_____

_____

Plot notes: _____

_____

_____

_____

_____

_____

Character notes: _____

_____

_____

_____

_____

Favorite quotes: _____

_____

_____

_____

_____

Other books to read by this author: _____

_____

DATE STARTED

/ /

DATE FINISHED

/ /

RATE THIS BOOK

☆ ☆ ☆ ☆ ☆

DATE STARTED

/ /

DATE FINISHED

/ /

RATE THIS BOOK

☆☆☆☆☆

BOOK TITLE:_____

_____

AUTHOR:_____

_____

_____

Plot notes: _____

_____

_____

_____

_____

_____

Character notes: _____

_____

_____

_____

_____

Favorite quotes: _____

_____

_____

_____

_____

Other books to read by this author: _____

_____

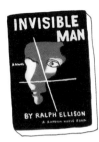

ICONIC COVERS

DATE STARTED

/   /

DATE FINISHED

/   /

RATE THIS BOOK

☆☆☆☆☆

BOOK TITLE:

AUTHOR:

Plot notes:

Character notes:

Favorite quotes:

Other books to read by this author:

BOOK TITLE: _____

_____

AUTHOR: _____

_____

_____

Plot notes: _____

_____

_____

_____

_____

Character notes: _____

_____

_____

_____

_____

Favorite quotes: _____

_____

_____

_____

_____

Other books to read by this author: _____

_____

DATE STARTED

/   /

DATE FINISHED

/   /

RATE THIS BOOK

☆ ☆ ☆ ☆ ☆

DATE STARTED

/   /

DATE FINISHED

/   /

RATE THIS BOOK

☆☆☆☆☆

BOOK TITLE: _____

_____

AUTHOR: _____

_____

Plot notes: _____

_____

_____

_____

_____

Character notes: _____

_____

_____

_____

_____

Favorite quotes: _____

_____

_____

_____

Other books to read by this author: _____

_____

BOOK TITLE: _____

_____

AUTHOR: _____

_____

_____

Plot notes: _____

_____

_____

_____

_____

Character notes: _____

_____

_____

_____

Favorite quotes: _____

_____

_____

_____

Other books to read by this author: _____

_____

BOOK TITLE:

AUTHOR:

Plot notes:

Character notes:

Favorite quotes:

Other books to read by this author:

DATE STARTED

/   /

DATE FINISHED

/   /

RATE THIS BOOK

☆☆☆☆☆

BOOK TITLE:

AUTHOR:

Plot notes:

Character notes:

Favorite quotes:

Other books to read by this author:

BOOK TITLE: _____

_____

AUTHOR: _____

_____

Plot notes: _____

_____

_____

_____

_____

Character notes: _____

_____

_____

_____

_____

Favorite quotes: _____

_____

_____

_____

_____

Other books to read by this author: _____

_____

DATE STARTED

/   /

DATE FINISHED

/   /

RATE THIS BOOK

☆ ☆ ☆ ☆ ☆

DATE STARTED

/ /

DATE FINISHED

/ /

RATE THIS BOOK

☆☆☆☆☆

BOOK TITLE:_____

_____

AUTHOR:_____

_____

_____

Plot notes: _____

_____

_____

_____

_____

_____

Character notes: _____

_____

_____

_____

_____

Favorite quotes: _____

_____

_____

_____

_____

Other books to read by this author: _____

_____

BOOK TITLE:

AUTHOR:

Plot notes:

Character notes:

Favorite quotes:

Other books to read by this author:

DATE STARTED

/   /

DATE FINISHED

/   /

RATE THIS BOOK

☆ ☆ ☆ ☆ ☆

DATE STARTED

/ /

DATE FINISHED

/ /

RATE THIS BOOK

☆☆☆☆☆

BOOK TITLE:

AUTHOR:

Plot notes:

Character notes:

Favorite quotes:

Other books to read by this author:

BOOKMOBILES & MORE

Il Bibliomotocarro
Basilicata, Italy

La Carreta Literaria
Cartagena de Indias, Colombia

MONKEY'S PAW
BIBLIO-MAT
OLD & UNUSUAL
EVERY BOOK A SURPRISE
NO TWO ALIKE
COLLECT ALL 112 MILLION TITLES

Biblio-mat at the Monkey's Paw
Toronto, Ottawa, Canada

The Garden Library for Refugees and Migrant Workers
Tel Aviv, Israel

BIBLIOBURRO

Biblioburro
Magdalena, Colombia

Tell a Story

Tell a Story
Lisbon, Portugal

DATE STARTED

/ /

DATE FINISHED

/ /

RATE THIS BOOK

☆☆☆☆☆

BOOK TITLE: _____

_____

AUTHOR: _____

_____

_____

Plot notes: _____

_____

_____

_____

_____

_____

Character notes: _____

_____

_____

_____

_____

Favorite quotes: _____

_____

_____

_____

_____

Other books to read by this author: _____

_____

BOOK TITLE: _____

_____

AUTHOR: _____

_____

_____

Plot notes: _____

_____

_____

_____

_____

Character notes: _____

_____

_____

_____

_____

Favorite quotes: _____

_____

_____

_____

_____

Other books to read by this author: _____

_____

DATE STARTED

/   /

DATE FINISHED

/   /

RATE THIS BOOK

☆☆☆☆☆

DATE STARTED

/   /

DATE FINISHED

/   /

RATE THIS BOOK

☆☆☆☆☆

BOOK TITLE: _____

_____

AUTHOR: _____

_____

_____

Plot notes: _____

_____

_____

_____

_____

_____

Character notes: _____

_____

_____

_____

_____

Favorite quotes: _____

_____

_____

_____

_____

Other books to read by this author: _____

_____

BOOK TITLE: _____

_____

AUTHOR: _____

_____

_____

Plot notes: _____

_____

_____

_____

_____

Character notes: _____

_____

_____

_____

Favorite quotes: _____

_____

_____

_____

Other books to read by this author: _____

_____

Coralie Bickford-Smith designed the Penguin Clothbound series, a large set of foil-stamped, cloth-covered classic books, each featuring a pattern of symbolic imagery from the story.

Yes, the text is upside down! Get it?

BEAUTIFUL CONTEMPORARY COVERS

BOOK TITLE: _____

_____

AUTHOR: _____

_____

_____

Plot notes: _____

_____

_____

_____

_____

_____

Character notes: _____

_____

_____

_____

_____

Favorite quotes: _____

_____

_____

_____

_____

Other books to read by this author: _____

_____

DATE STARTED

/   /

DATE FINISHED

/   /

RATE THIS BOOK

☆ ☆ ☆ ☆ ☆

DATE STARTED

/   /

DATE FINISHED

/   /

RATE THIS BOOK

☆☆☆☆☆

BOOK TITLE:

AUTHOR:

Plot notes:

Character notes:

Favorite quotes:

Other books to read by this author:

BOOK TITLE: _____

_____

AUTHOR: _____

_____

_____

Plot notes: _____

_____

_____

_____

_____

Character notes: _____

_____

_____

_____

_____

Favorite quotes: _____

_____

_____

_____

_____

Other books to read by this author: _____

_____

DATE STARTED

/   /

DATE FINISHED

/   /

RATE THIS BOOK

☆ ☆ ☆ ☆ ☆

BOOKS TO CHECK OUT

BOOKS TO CHECK OUT

Book title: _____

Author: _____

Notes: _____

_____

_____

Book title: _____

Author: _____

Notes: _____

_____

_____

Book title: _____

Author: _____

Notes: _____

_____

_____

Book title: _____

Author: _____

Notes: _____

_____

_____

BOOKS TO CHECK OUT

Book title: _____
Author: _____
Notes: _____
_____
_____
_____

Book title: _____
Author: _____
Notes: _____
_____
_____
_____

Book title: _____
Author: _____
Notes: _____
_____
_____
_____

Book title: _____
Author: _____
Notes: _____
_____
_____

Nº 1

Nº 2

Nº 3

Nº 4

Nº 5

Nº 6

Nº 7

Nº 8

Nº 9

Nº 10

ALL-TIME BEST SELLERS

BOOKS TO CHECK OUT

Book title: _____

Author: _____

Notes: _____

_____

_____

Book title: _____

Author: _____

Notes: _____

_____

_____

Book title: _____

Author: _____

Notes: _____

_____

_____

Book title: _____

Author: _____

Notes: _____

_____

BOOKS TO CHECK OUT

Book title: _____

Author: _____

Notes: _____

_____

_____

Book title: _____

Author: _____

Notes: _____

_____

_____

Book title: _____

Author: _____

Notes: _____

_____

_____

Book title: _____

Author: _____

Notes: _____

_____

_____

BOOKS TO CHECK OUT

Book title: _____

Author: _____

Notes: _____

_____

_____

_____

Book title: _____

Author: _____

Notes: _____

_____

_____

_____

Book title: _____

Author: _____

Notes: _____

_____

_____

_____

Book title: _____

Author: _____

Notes: _____

_____

_____

BOOKS TO CHECK OUT

Book title: _____

Author: _____

Notes: _____

_____

_____

Book title: _____

Author: _____

Notes: _____

_____

_____

Book title: _____

Author: _____

Notes: _____

_____

_____

Book title: _____

Author: _____

Notes: _____

_____

BOOKS TO CHECK OUT

Book title: _____

Author: _____

Notes: _____

_____

_____

_____

Book title: _____

Author: _____

Notes: _____

_____

_____

_____

Book title: _____

Author: _____

Notes: _____

_____

_____

_____

Book title: _____

Author: _____

Notes: _____

_____

_____

BOOKS TO CHECK OUT

Book title: _____

Author: _____

Notes: _____

_____

_____

_____

Book title: _____

Author: _____

Notes: _____

_____

_____

Book title: _____

Author: _____

Notes: _____

_____

_____

Book title: _____

Author: _____

Notes: _____

_____

_____

BOOKS TO CHECK OUT

Book title: _____

Author: _____

Notes: _____

_____

_____

Book title: _____

Author: _____

Notes: _____

_____

_____

Book title: _____

Author: _____

Notes: _____

_____

_____

Book title: _____

Author: _____

Notes: _____

_____

_____

BOOKS TO CHECK OUT

Book title: _____

Author: _____

Notes: _____

_____

_____

Book title: _____

Author: _____

Notes: _____

_____

_____

Book title: _____

Author: _____

Notes: _____

_____

_____

Book title: _____

Author: _____

Notes: _____

_____

_____

BOOKS TO CHECK OUT

Book title: _____

Author: _____

Notes: _____

_____

_____

Book title: _____

Author: _____

Notes: _____

_____

_____

Book title: _____

Author: _____

Notes: _____

_____

_____

Book title: _____

Author: _____

Notes: _____

_____

_____

BOOKS TO CHECK OUT

Book title: _____

Author: _____

Notes: _____

_____

_____

Book title: _____

Author: _____

Notes: _____

_____

_____

Book title: _____

Author: _____

Notes: _____

_____

_____

Book title: _____

Author: _____

Notes: _____

_____

IDEAS & INSPIRATIONS

IDEAS & INSPIRATIONS

Ever had an "aha!" moment while deep into a book?
Record brilliant bits and clever quotes all in one place.

DAVID
MITCHELL
cloud
atlas

IDEAS & INSPIRATIONS

IDEAS & INSPIRATIONS

IDEAS & INSPIRATIONS

New York Times bestseller

The Girls
a novel
Emma Cline

IDEAS & INSPIRATIONS

ZADIE
SMITH
ON
BEAUTY

A NOVEL
AUTHOR OF "WHITE TEETH"

READING
RECOMMENDATIONS

CLOUD ATLAS — David Mitchell

bel canto — Ann Patchett

HARUKI MURAKAMI — THE WIND-UP BIRD CHRONICLE

The God of Small Things — Arundhati Roy

GILEAD | MARILYNNE ROBINSON — PICADOR

MICHAEL CHABON — the AMAZING ADVENTURES OF KAVALIER & CLAY

THE FORTRESS OF SOLITUDE — JONATHAN LETHEM — A NOVEL — VINTAGE

THE SAVAGE DETECTIVES — ROBERTO BOLAÑO — PICADOR

EVERYTHING IS ILLUMINATED — JONATHAN SAFRAN FOER

mark haddon — the curious incident of the dog in the night-time

The Poisonwood Bible — a novel — BARBARA KINGSOLVER

NEVER LET ME GO — KAZUO ISHIGURO

A FINE BALANCE — MISTRY — VINTAGE

THE LOVELY BONES — ALICE SEBOLD — Little, Brown

Yann Martel — Life of Pi

WHITE TEETH ZADIE SMITH — WHITE TEETH ZADIE SMITH — WHITE TEETH ZADIE SMITH — WHITE TEETH ZADIE SMITH — VINTAGE

FIGHT CLUB >> CHUCK PALAHNIUK — NORTON

jhumpa lahiri — the namesake

IAN McEWAN — ATONEMENT

PHILIP ROTH — THE HUMAN STAIN — VINTAGE

david foster wallace — infinite jest — BACK BAY

MIDDLESEX — JEFFREY EUGENIDES — PICADOR

READING RECOMMENDATIONS

The last page, the last line—how bittersweet it is to finish a book! Choosing your next read is the only salve. If you don't have a new book on deck, here's a sampling of inspired lists that any bibliophile will enjoy. These lists are by no means exhaustive, but perhaps your new favorite book will be among them.

BOOK CLUB DARLINGS

The Elegance of the Hedgehog, Muriel Barbery
The Mothers, Brit Bennett
Behind the Beautiful Forevers, Katherine Boo
Room, Emma Donoghue
Eleanor Oliphant Is Completely Fine, Gail Honeyman
An American Marriage, Tayari Jones
The History of Love, Nicole Krauss
The Paris Wife, Paula McLain
The Bluest Eye, Toni Morrison
A Tale for the Time Being, Ruth Ozeki
State of Wonder, Ann Patchett
Lucky Boy, Shanthi Sekaran
Where'd You Go, Bernadette?, Maria Semple
Olive Kitteridge, Elizabeth Strout
The Rules of Civility, Amor Towles

CULT CLASSICS

The Hitchhiker's Guide to the Galaxy, Douglas Adams
Ficciones, Jorge Luis Borges
Invisible Cities, Italo Calvino
The Alchemist, Paulo Coelho
House of Leaves, Mark Danielewski
Geek Love, Katherine Dunn
The Princess Bride, William Goldman
We Have Always Lived in the Castle, Shirley Jackson

Pale Fire, Vladimir Nabokov
Zen and the Art of Motorcycle Maintenance, Robert Pirsig
Valley of the Dolls, Jacqueline Susann
Perfume, Patrick Süskind
A Confederacy of Dunces, John Kennedy Toole
Cat's Cradle, Kurt Vonnegut

ESSAYS

I'm Judging You, Luvvie Ajayi
Known and Strange Things, Teju Cole
I Was Told There'd Be Cake, Sloane Crosley
Slouching Toward Bethlehem, Joan Didion
I Feel Bad about My Neck, Nora Ephron
Discontent and Its Civilizations: Dispatches from Lahore, New York, and London, Mohsin Hamid
Arguably, Christopher Hitchens
We Are Never Meeting in Real Life, Samantha Irby
The Empathy Exams, Leslie Jamison
The Control of Nature, John McPhee
Me Talk Pretty One Day, David Sedaris
Tiny Beautiful Things: Advice on Love and Life from Dear Sugar, Cheryl Strayed
Men Explain Things to Me, Rebecca Solnit
A Supposedly Fun Thing I'll Never Do Again, David Foster Wallace

FANTASY

The Last Unicorn, Peter S. Beagle
The Neverending Story, Michael Ende
Stardust, Neil Gaiman
The Killing Moon, N. K. Jemisin
Howl's Moving Castle, Diana Wynne Jones
The Lion, the Witch, and the Wardrobe, C. S. Lewis
A Game of Thrones, George R. R. Martin
Dragonflight, Anne McCaffrey

(continued)

The Dark Is Rising
by Susan Cooper

"I read it as a kid, and it has stuck with me. As an adult I have reread the whole series and listened to the audio-book several times, and it still is as enjoy-able as the first time."

Atheneum 1972
hardcover, art by
Alan E. Cober

—Julia Hobart, *Bookbuyer at the Bookloft in Great Barrington, Massachusetts, USA*

Oryx and Crake
by Margaret Atwood

"A dystopian novel set in the near future, a *Brave New World* for the 21st century. Both a love story and a story of total destruc-tion, in which one man struggles to survive in a world where it seems everyone else has been killed by a plague. A terrifying vision of what could happen if we allow greed to take genetic engineering to an unimaginable end. All this plus it is funny often, since we humans are."

Bloomsbury 2009
hardcover, design
by David Mann, art
by Victoria Sawdon

—Sandi Torkildson, *Co-owner of A Room of One's Own, Madison, Wisconsin, USA*

Matilda
by Roald Dahl

"My favorite book of all time is *Matilda* by Roald Dahl. I was already an established 'reader' by the time it found me, but it really served to solidify that identity for life (I now have a Matilda tattoo!). Matilda

was able to find solace and magic through books and learning, and she was able to move past dreary days (and insufferable parents and principals) through her smarts. And don't we all dream of going off to live with Miss Honey in a little cottage full of books?"

Viking Kestrel 1988
hardcover, art by
Quentin Blake

—Maris Kreizman, *Editorial director of Book of the Month*

The Song of the Dodo
by David Quammen

"Quammen superbly blends exquisite biographies of Charles Darwin and his nemesis and underdog Alfred Wallace with fascinat-ing accounts of strange, contemporary creatures

Scribner 1997
paperback, design by
Calvin Chou, art
by Walter Ford

whose existential vulnerability is a real warning to each of us about the con-sequences of habitat destruction."

— Adah Fitzgerald, *Owner of Main Street Books in Davidson, North Carolina, USA*

FANTASY (CONTINUED)

The Colour of Magic, Terry Pratchett
The Golden Compass, Philip Pullman
The Way of Kings, Brandon Sanderson
The Hobbit, J. R. R. Tolkien
The Once and Future King, T. H. White

FOOD WRITING

Kitchen Confidential, Anthony Bourdain
Heat, Bill Buford
My Life in France, Julia Child & Alex Prud'homme
Home Cooking, Laurie Colwin
The Art of Eating, M. F. K. Fisher
Blood, Bones & Butter, Gabrielle Hamilton
Climbing the Mango Trees, Madhur Jaffrey
Animal Vegetable Mineral: A Year of Food Life, Barbara Kingsolver
Relish: My Life in the Kitchen, Lucy Knisley
The Sweet Life in Paris, David Lebovitz
Adventures on the Wine Route, Kermit Lynch
Tender at the Bone, Ruth Reichl
The Kitchen Diaries, Nigel Slater
The Cooking Gene, Michael W. Twitty

MEMOIRS

I Know Why the Caged Bird Sings, Maya Angelou
The Diving Bell and the Butterfly, Jean-Dominique Bauby
Wild Swans, Jung Chang
A Heartbreaking Work of Staggering Genius, Dave Eggers
The Liars' Club, Mary Karr
Heart Berries, Terese Marie Mailhot
Black Swan Green, David Mitchell
The Argonauts, Maggie Nelson
Persepolis, Marjane Satrapi

Just Kids, Patti Smith
First They Killed My Father, Loung Ung
Night, Elie Wiesel
Oranges Are Not the Only Fruit, Jeanette Winterson
Brown Girl Dreaming, Jacqueline Woodson

MYSTERIES

The Big Sleep, Raymond Chandler
The Black Echo, Michael Connelly
In the Woods, Tana French
The Maltese Falcon, Dashiell Hammett
The Talented Mr. Ripley, Patricia Highsmith
Smilla's Sense of Snow, Peter Høeg
An Unsuitable Job for a Woman, P. D. James
Firewall, Henning Mankell
The Redbreast, Jo Nesbø
Bury Your Dead, Louise Penny
The Laughing Policeman, Maj Sjöwall & Per Wahlöö
The Intuitionist, Colson Whitehead

NOVELS OF THE 1800S

Pride & Prejudice, Jane Austen
Jane Eyre, Charlotte Brontë
Wuthering Heights, Emily Brontë
A Tale of Two Cities, Charles Dickens
Crime and Punishment, Fyodor Dostoevsky
The Count of Monte Cristo, Alexandre Dumas
Middlemarch, George Eliot
Les Miserables, Victor Hugo
Moby Dick, Herman Melville
Frankenstein, Mary Shelley
Dracula, Bram Stoker
Vanity Fair, William Makepeace Thackeray

Knopf
1986 hardcover

Anagrams
by Lorrie Moore

"Anagrams broke apart all my expectations about what a novel could do. As you might guess from the book's title, it presents many different versions of its wonderfully flawed heroine, and maintains a delicate balance between funny and sad. It is eminently quotable, and it is definitive proof that puns can be profound."

—Maris Kreizman, *Editorial director of Book of the Month*

Bad Feminist
by Roxane Gay

Harper Perennial
2014 paperback,
design by
Robin Bilardello

"In *Bad Feminist* Roxane Gay blends personal narrative with brilliant, often hilarious critiques of pop culture and politics. She claims the messy contradictions within both the movement and herself. She stares down and shreds apart the feminist killjoy stereotype using all the tools in her belt—irony, vulnerability, jokes, and just plain common sense."

—Sarah Hollenbeck, *Co-owner of Women & Children First in Chicago, Illinois, USA*

The Turner House
by Angela Flournoy

Houghton Mifflin
Harcourt 2015
hardcover, design by
Martha Kennedy

"Officially, this book is about a family with 13 grown children figuring out what to do with the family home on Detroit's East Side as property values deteriorate and parents age and die. Also race and class and addiction and love and belief and the supernatural and mental health and manhood and womanhood and forgiveness. But here's what I love most about it: Often when I read a book that weaves together past and present stories and several perspectives, there are some I like less and slog through to get back to the better ones. In *The Turner House*, I was always excited to read what came next, only slowing down to try and spend more time with these characters. It feels like every single person is real, living and breathing out there, each one flawed—difficult, dishonest, failing, flailing—and yet so wholly engaging. I loved them even when I didn't like them."

—Rachel Fershleiser, *Internet-enabled literary enthusiast*

BOOKISH PEOPLE RECOMMEND

A Madman Dreams of Turing Machines
by Janna Levin

Anchor 2007 paperback, design by Peter Mendelsund

"The ideas of mathematician Kurt Gödel and computing pioneer Alan Turing fundamentally unsettled and reshaped modern life. Astrophysicist and author Janna Levin—one of the most poetic prose writers of our time—twines their parallel lives into a stunning novel exploring the limits of logic, the elusive nature of truth, and the roiling relationship between genius and madness."

—Maria Popova, *reader, writer, and founder of brainpickings.org*

The Honest Truth
by Dan Gemeinhart

Scholastic 2015 hardcover, design and art by Nina Goffi

"Kids often dream of running away from home. In *The Honest Truth*, Mark plans out an elaborate trip that will take him and his dog Beau away from their home to one of the tallest mountains in Washington State. As the book progresses, readers slowly begin to realize that Mark's journey to the mountain might be the last thing he ever does."

—Colby Sharp, *fifth-grade teacher in Parma, Michigan, USA, and author of* The Creativity Project

The Zuni Cafe Cookbook
by Judy Rodgers

W. W. Norton & Company 2002 hardcover, photo by Gentl & Hyers/Edge

"*The Zuni Cafe Cookbook* is the cookbook I love and recommend most. It tells you why you're doing what you're doing in the kitchen in a concise yet poetic way. It's the kind of book you want to take to bed with you and read all night. You learn what a dish should sound like when it's ready—how the sizzle slows or speeds up. How a syrup feels on the spoon when it's done."

—Celia Sack, *owner of Omnivore Books on Food, San Francisco, California, USA*

Gabi, a Girl in Pieces
by Isabel Quintero

Cinco Puntos Press 2014 paperback, design and art by Zeke Peña

"*Gabi, a Girl in Pieces* is a book I wished I had as a teen. Gabi is a loud, fat, budding poet who is constantly trying to meet the expectations of her mother, friends, and school counselors. Her journal entries could've been my diary entries at age 18, when I was trying to find the right balance between meeting my single mother's expectations and juggling my place in two worlds—the American one and the traditional Dominican one."

—Shelley M. Diaz, *reviews manager and editor at School Library Journal*

NOVELS OF THE 21ST CENTURY

Americanah, Chimamanda Ngozi Adichie
The Sellout, Paul Beatty
The Brief Wondrous Life of Oscar Wao, Junot Díaz
All the Light We Cannot See, Anthony Doerr
What Is the What, Dave Eggers
The Round House, Louise Erdrich
Homegoing, Yaa Gyasi
A Sleepwalker's Guide to Dancing, Mira Jacobs
Pachinko, Min Jin Lee
Little Fires Everywhere, Celeste Ng
The Sympathizer, Viet Thanh Nguyen
There There, Tommy Orange
Absurdistan, Gary Shteyngart
The Goldfinch, Donna Tartt
The Underground Railroad, Colson Whitehead

SHORT STORIES

What It Means When a Man Falls from the Sky, Lesley Nneka Arimah
Bloodchild and Other Stories, Octavia Butler
Stories, Anton Chekhov
Stories of Your Life and Others, Ted Chiang
Dubliners, James Joyce
Interpreter of Maladies, Jhumpa Lahiri
Get in Trouble, Kelly Link
Her Body and Other Parties, Carmen Machado
Birds of America, Lorrie Moore
Runaway, Alice Munro
The Complete Stories, Flannery O'Connor
What Is Not Yours Is Not Yours, Helen Oyeyemi
St. Lucy's Home for Girls Raised by Wolves, Karen Russell